I am a
Dentist

Deborah Chancellor

W

This edition 2012

First published in 2010
by Franklin Watts

Copyright © Franklin Watts 2010

Franklin Watts
338 Euston Road
London NW1 3BH

Franklin Watts Australia
Level 17/207 Kent Street
Sydney, NSW 2000

Series editor: Jeremy Smith
Art director: Jonathan Hair
Design: Elaine Wilkinson
Photography: Chris Fairclough

Every attempt has been made to clear copyright. Should there be any inadvertent omission please
apply to the publisher for rectification.

Thanks to Chris, Donna, Katharine, Angela, Lily, Archie, Tracy, Connor, Scarlett, Louis and
all the staff at Broxbourne Dental Care.

Dewey number: 617.6

ISBN: 978 1 4451 0903 9

Printed in China

Franklin Watts is a division of Hachette Children's Books,
an Hachette UK company.
www.hachette.co.uk

Contents

Words in **bold** are in the glossary on page 24.

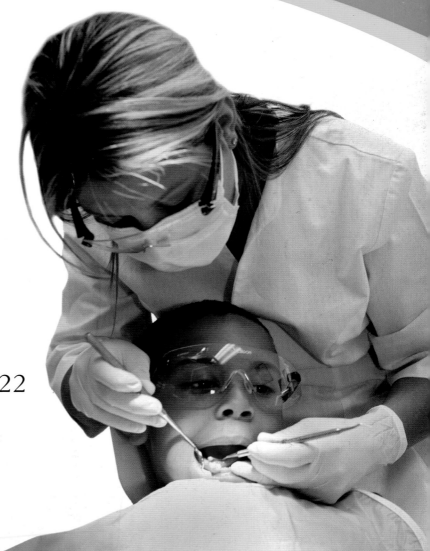

My job

I am a dentist. I check people's teeth, to see if they are strong and healthy.

What do you think?

Why do people go to the dentist?

4

I work at a **dental surgery** in a town
called Broxbourne.

At reception

People who want to see me have to phone the receptionist at the surgery to make an appointment.

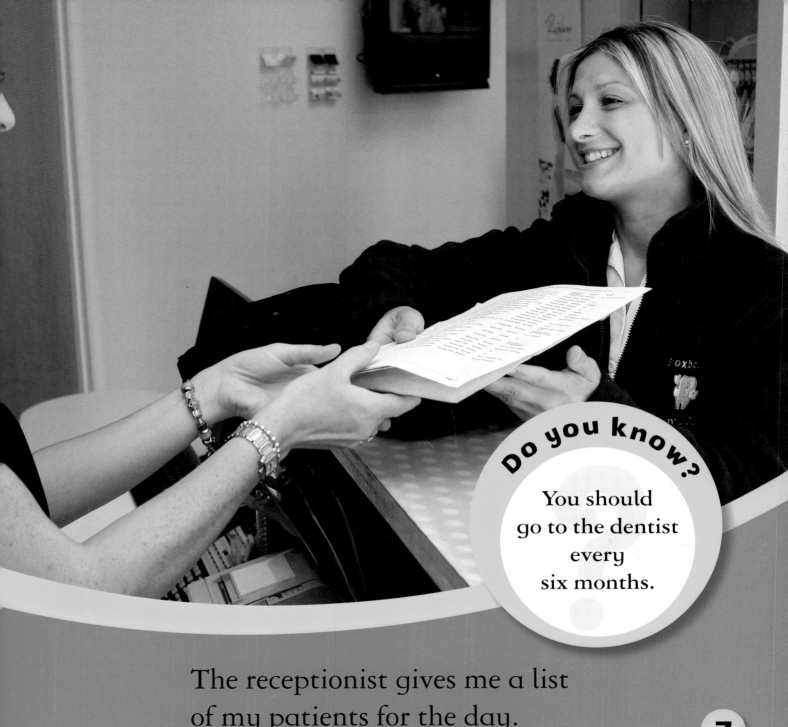

Do you know?

You should go to the dentist every six months.

The receptionist gives me a list of my patients for the day.

In my surgery

I have lots of special equipment in my room at the dental surgery.

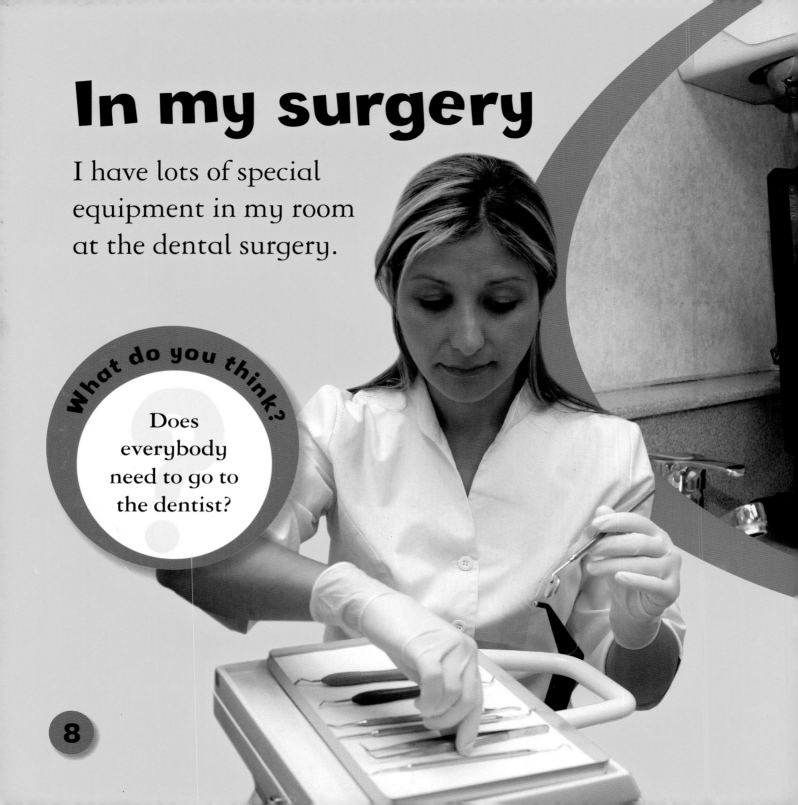

What do you think?

Does everybody need to go to the dentist?

All my patients' dental **records**
are on the computer.

The waiting room

Patients wait in the waiting room.
There are books for children to read.

My dental nurse fetches the patients when it is their turn to see me.

What do you think?

Do you like going to the dentist? Why?

My dental nurse

My dental nurse asks the patient to sit in a special chair. It moves up, down, forwards and backwards!

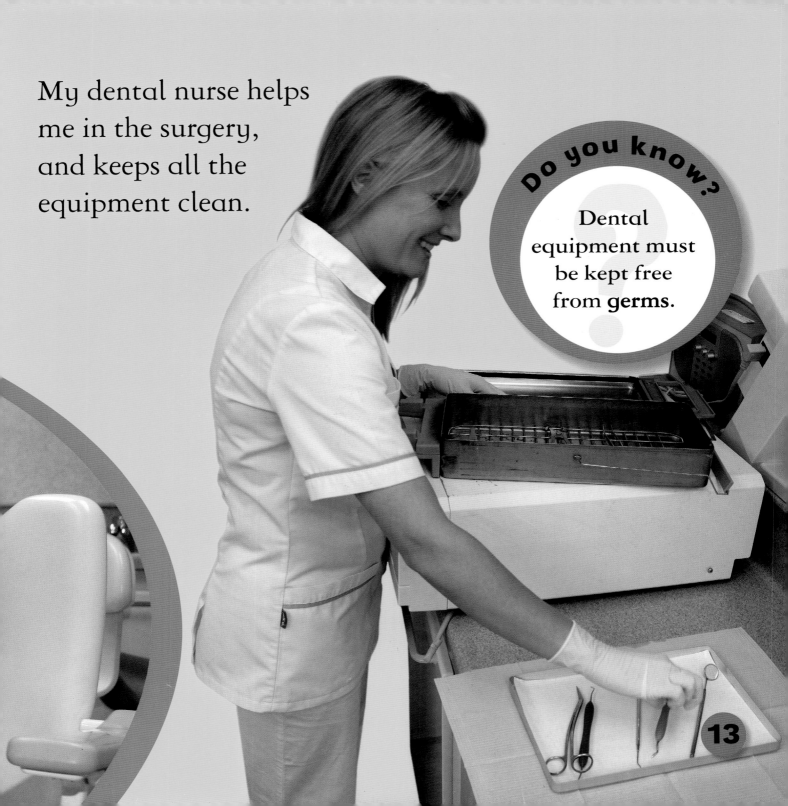

My dental nurse helps me in the surgery, and keeps all the equipment clean.

Do you know?

Dental equipment must be kept free from **germs**.

13

Check-up

I put a tiny camera in my patient's mouth, so I can see if their teeth and **gums** are healthy.

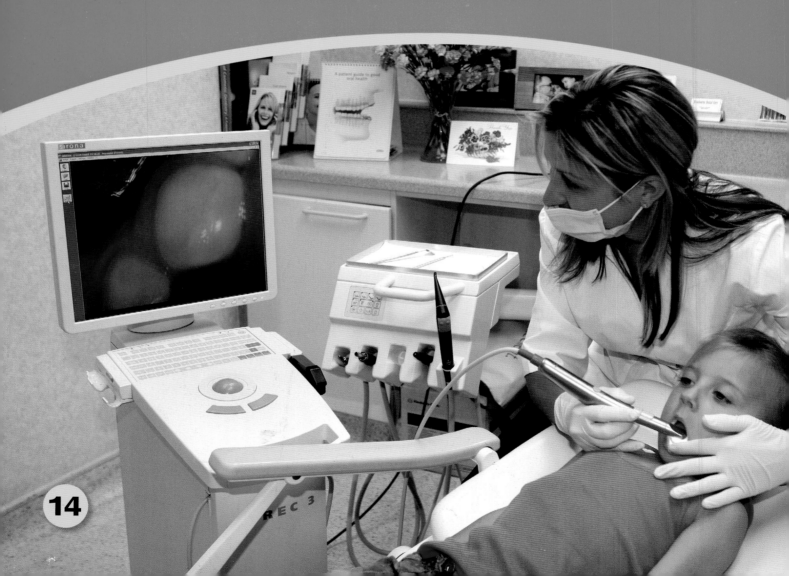

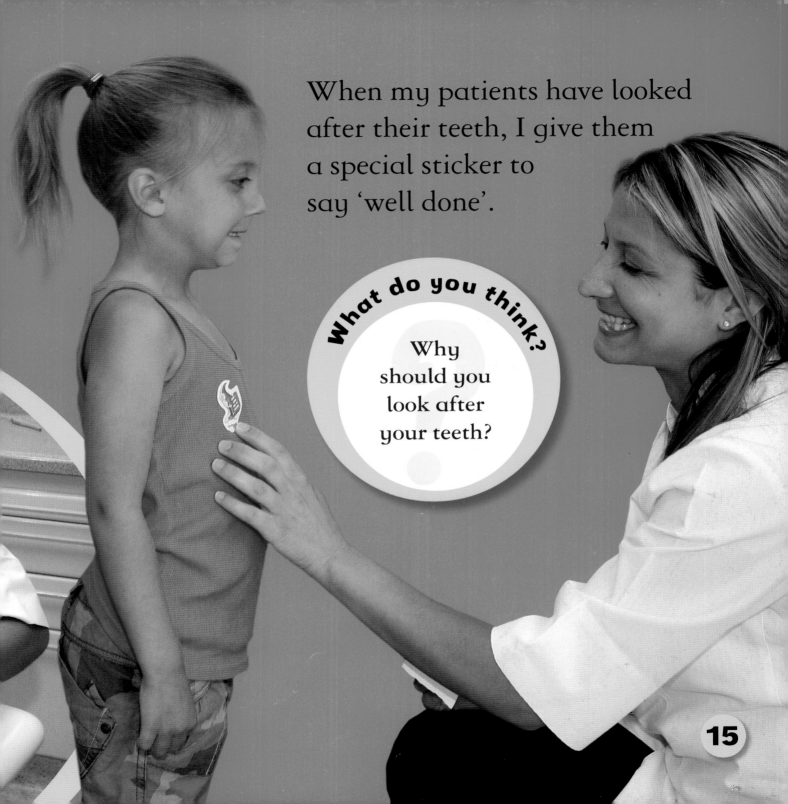

When my patients have looked after their teeth, I give them a special sticker to say 'well done'.

What do you think?

Why should you look after your teeth?

X-ray

I give some patients an **x-ray**, so I can see what **treatment** they need.

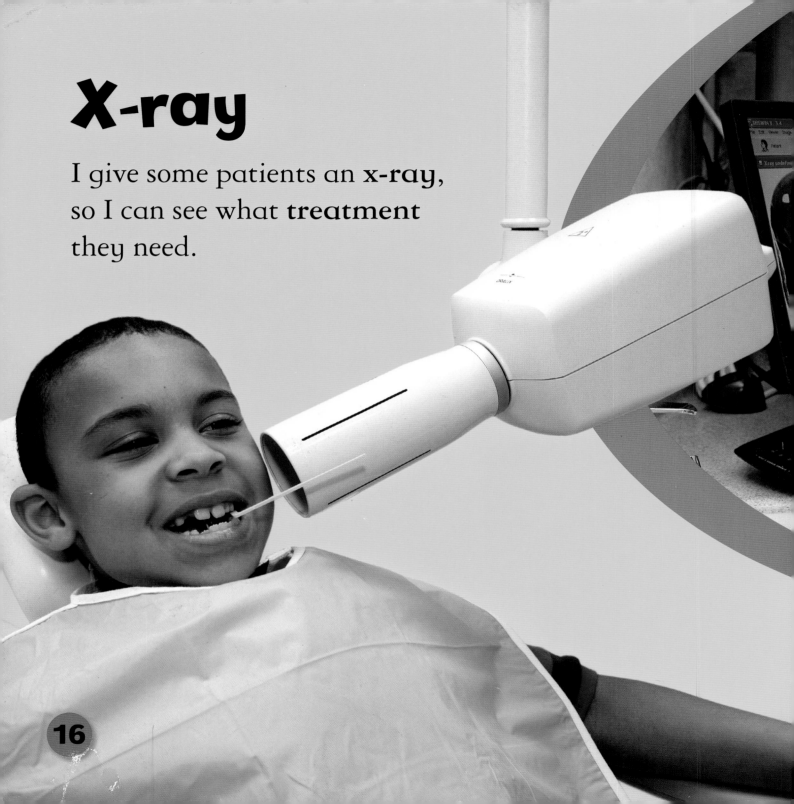

What do you think?

Would you like to work at a dental surgery one day? Why?

We look at the x-ray on the computer, and talk about it together.

Fillings

If a patient has **tooth decay**, I give them a filling. First, I prepare the mixture for the filling.

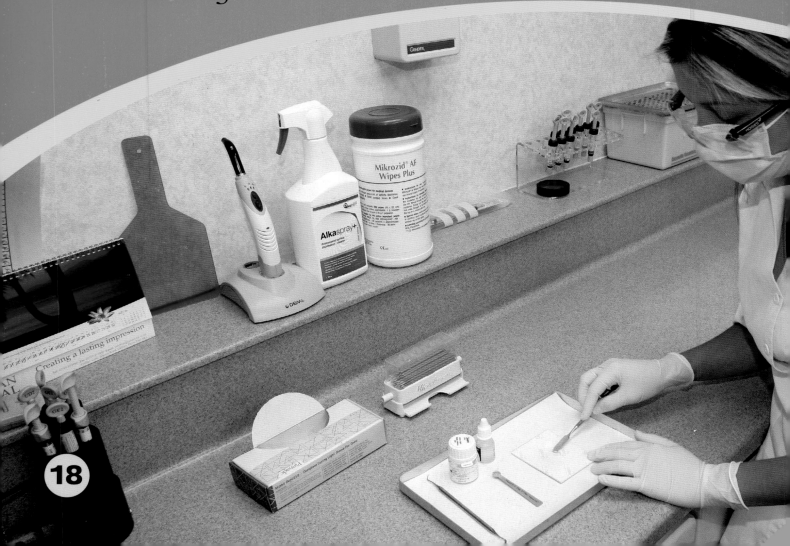

Then, I fill the hole in their tooth with the mixture.
This stops the tooth from hurting.

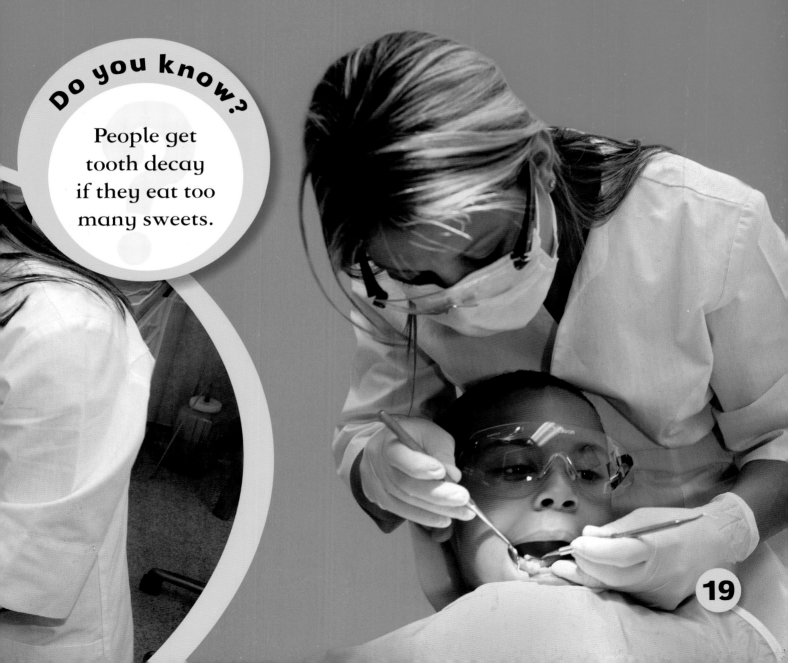

Do you know?

People get tooth decay if they eat too many sweets.

19

Accident!

Sometimes, people come to the surgery after an accident. They may have lost a tooth.

I see them straight away and give them **emergency** treatment.

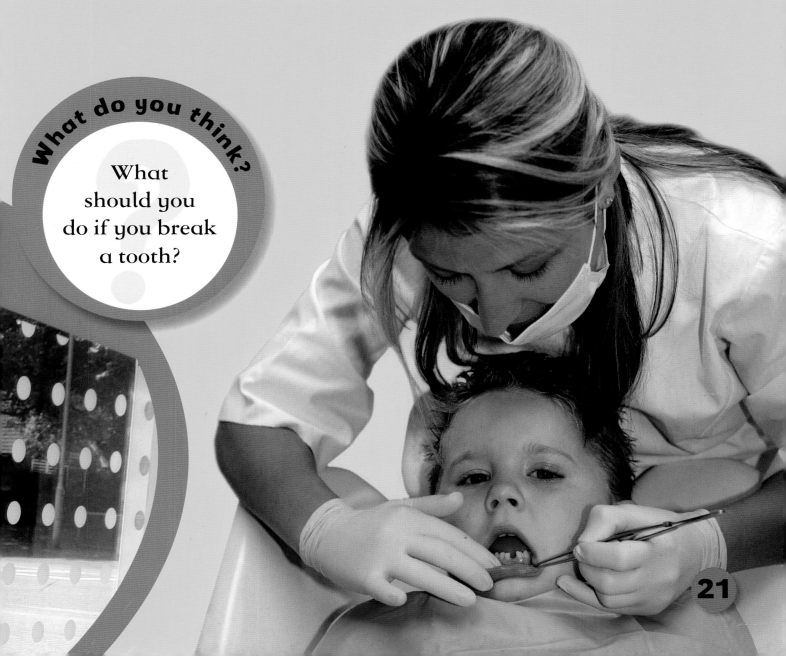

What do you think?

What should you do if you break a tooth?

21

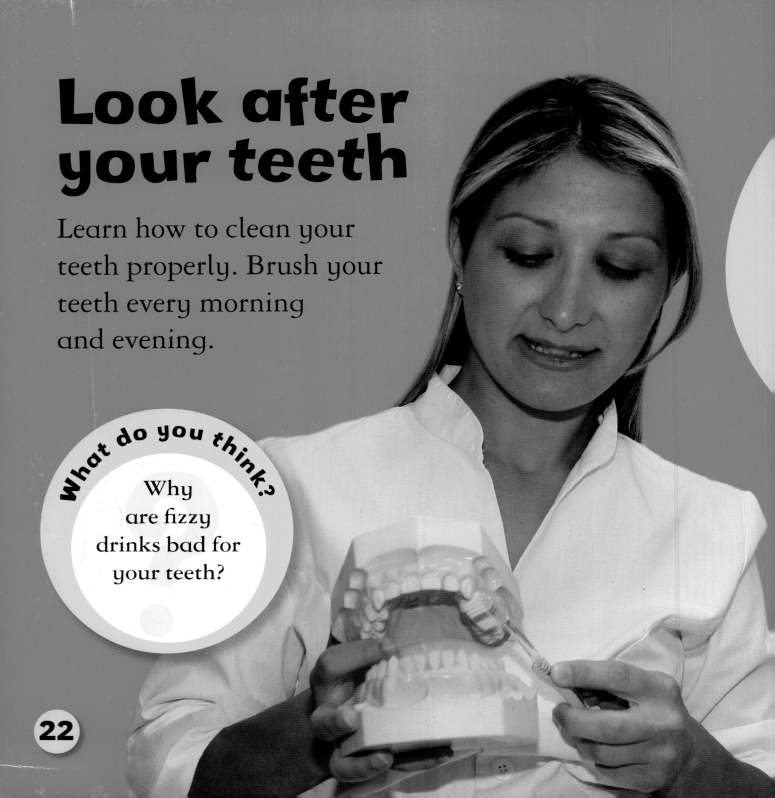

Look after your teeth

Learn how to clean your teeth properly. Brush your teeth every morning and evening.

What do you think?

Why are fizzy drinks bad for your teeth?

Choose food and drinks that are good for your teeth such as fruit and milk.

23

Glossary

dental nurse someone who helps dentists in a surgery

dental records information about your teeth and gums

dental surgery a place where dentists work

emergency a sudden, dangerous situation

germs things that cause disease

gums the part of your mouth that holds your teeth

tooth decay part of a tooth that is rotting away

treatment the care you are given to make you better

x-ray a photo that shows your bones and teeth

Index